Personal Branding Secrets for Beginners:
A Short and Simple Guide to Getting Started with Your Personal Brand

By
Mary Lou Kayser

www.MaryLouKayser.com

Personal Branding Secrets for Beginners by Mary Lou Kayser. Published by Blue Ink Publishing c/o The Kingfisher Group, 10260 SW Greenburg Road, Ste. 400, Portland, Oregon 97223

www.maryloukayser.com

mlk@maryloukayser.com

Cover by 3fatbirds. Image credit Big Stock Photo.

Printed in the United States of America

ISBN-13: 978-0692222645

Digital version available on Kindle and other devices.

3   2   1

DEDICATION

For Ginna and Ben. Thanks for being my originals.

To Emma + Dallas,
HERE's to Being
authentically, wonderfully
yourselves!
Mly

"Be yourself. The world worships the original."
Ingrid Bergman

Contents

Preface to the Third Edition

When I first wrote *Personal Branding Secrets for Beginners* in late 2011, the online scene was just beginning to take off. Twitter, Facebook, YouTube and LinkedIn had all made it to the five year mark or beyond. The tipping point of activity on these giant social media platforms was just about to hit.

In many ways, we have the rise of the Internet to thank for the need to develop our personal brands. Like it or not, a personal brand has become an integral part of today's professional landscape.

As I write the preface to the third edition of this book, we are in the first quarter of 2016. From this vantage point, not only is personal branding important to today's professional, but it is also absolutely imperative for anyone who is serious about growing their business or career to take the process of personal branding seriously.

The world is getting noisier and more crowded every day. Knowing who you are, what you stand for, and the value you bring to the world can help you to cut through the clutter and get noticed for something that matters to you, and in turn, serve an audience that desires what you offer it.

As that wonderful old proverb goes:

"The best time to plant a tree is 20 years ago. The second-best time is now."

Here's to planting your personal branding tree and seeing it flourish!

Mary Lou Kayser
Portland, Oregon
March 2016

Introduction

"Too many people overvalue what they are not and undervalue what they are."
Malcolm Forbes

Mention certain names in passing conversation and people instantly know who you're talking about. Names like Sir Richard Branson. Michael Jordan. Bill Gates. Oprah.

Whether made up of one word or two, these names stand for something beyond the person to whom they belong:

- Michael Jordan = Basketball Greatness, Hanes Spokesman
- Bill Gates = Microsoft, Business Success, Philanthropist
- Oprah = Talk Show Queen, Generosity, Philanthropist, Career Changer for Authors
- Sir Richard Branson = Business Maverick, Visionary, Philanthropist
- Elon Musk=Technology Wizard, Innovator, Visionary

They are, essentially, the epitome of personal branding.

Personal branding is a big buzzword these days. You may be wondering what all the noise is about. What exactly is personal branding and why should you care?

For starters, you should care because in a noisy and cluttered world, the need for individuality has never been greater.

Secondly, if you don't take the time to design and define your personal brand, someone else will do it for you by default.

Finally, you need to control the creation of your personal brand because you are remarkable.

That's right! Let me say that again:

You are remarkable!

And creating your personal brand will allow you to project into the world what is remarkable about *you*.

That's what it takes to succeed today.

You have to stand out from the rest of the pack and be noticed. On your terms. In your own, unique way.

You don't have to be famous to benefit from personal branding. Many normal, everyday people are currently creating and building powerful personal brands that extend their reach, increase their value, and represent something bigger than themselves.

They made a conscious decision to take personal branding seriously because they understand that, at the end of the day, living a successful and satisfying life is grounded in moving yourself forward, day after day, year after year.

It's about who you are, what you do, and how the world interprets these two things.

Whether you work for yourself as an entrepreneur or you work for someone else, developing your personal brand is key for survival in today's tough economy.

But you can't do this alone.

This is where "Personal Branding Secrets for Beginners" comes in. It is a guide designed as an introduction to personal branding.

After several years of working with professionals from all walks of life, both online and offline, I noticed there was a need for a quick and handy overview of personal branding for people who have heard the term, but don't know much about it.

The following pages will quickly answer for you some of the most common questions about personal branding so that you can confidently and purposefully move forward with your own process of building a personal brand...and begin reaping the rewards.

This book is by no means a complete guide to personal branding. Rather, it's an introduction to some of the most common elements of personal branding anyone can grasp. At the end of the book, I have included a list of trusted resources for those readers who want more detailed information about personal branding.

The good news is, it's never too late to start developing your personal brand.

So...are you ready to get started on your journey into personal branding?

Onward!

Chapter 1: What Exactly Is a Personal Brand, Anyway?

"Life isn't about finding yourself. Life is about creating yourself."
George Bernhard Shaw

First, let me start with what a personal brand is NOT.

A personal brand is NOT your resume, or your degrees, or your job title. It isn't a logo or a slogan, either. While each of these things may reflect or represent elements of your personal brand, each in itself does not make up the whole that is the Brand Called You.

A personal brand is much bigger than a piece of paper or a cool symbol on the side of a shoe. It is a reflection of **who you are and what you value**. Some refer to a personal brand as a "personal value statement" – what *value* you bring to the world. This value could be rooted in a service you provide, or a set of skills you have, or a unique talent that you possess. The types of values are as varied as there are individuals.

Another way of looking at what your personal brand could be is through the lens of problems – specifically, what problems you can solve for others.

In a world always looking for answers, if your personal brand can become a solution to a problem, then you have succeeded.

Here is a simple example of a personal branding statement I generated for myself:

"Mary Lou Kayser is an innovative, nimble, and unassuming business strategist who helps emerging and established leaders create best-in-class assets so they can grow and profit in the global marketplace."

A general template for generating your own personal branding statement looks like this:

_____ (your name) is a _____ (book publisher, playwright, executive coach, etc.) who _____ (does something – make this active and other-focused) for _____ (your target audience) so they can _____

(here is where you identify the result of transformation your target audience experiences as a result of using your product or service).

When I work with my coaching clients, I walk them through a series of exercises like this one to help their personal brand emerge. Some people like to add a string of three adjectives before their role. Notice how I inserted the words "innovative," "nimble," and "unassuming" before "business strategist." Feel free to play around with this framework to fit your style and personality.

Another exercise that works well for people new to the personal branding concept is to spy on others who move in the same market space as you. What I mean when I say spy on them is to visit their websites, their social media profiles, or find articles they have written and read their "About Me" pages, summaries or bios. LinkedIn can be a great place for spying.

For example, say you are someone who helps companies with project management challenges, but aren't sure how to write up a personal branding statement. Open up LinkedIn, type "project manager" in the search bar, and look at various profiles of people who pop up with that title to get a sense of how you might write about yourself as a project management expert.

Here is a modified project manager's personal branding statement from LinkedIn. I've inserted a fictitious name for illustration purposes:

"Bob Smith has been in the Information Technology industry and a project manager for over 15 years. His contract consulting clients began with several global Fortune 50 companies during the Y2K surge and progressed toward the entrepreneurial start-ups and emerging enterprises. In recent years, he's been an equity partner in several start-up projects.

"Today, Bob helps entrepreneurial leaders (in a one on one format) assess their current situation, facilitate their creation of strategic plans and assist in implementation of efficient systems at a tactical level to secure growth and stability for their businesses."

You can learn a lot about different styles and ways of crafting a personal branding statement by looking at what others have done. This particular example makes it clear to the reader who Bob Smith is, what challenges he helps others solve, and who he works with. I don't recommend ever copying anyone else's branding statement and then merely substituting your name and details into it, but learning what is possible from others is definitely okay.

A small business owner's personal branding statement might look something like this:

"Through her intuition and genuine concern for- and interest in – others, Jane Hanson builds long-lasting, fruitful relationships with her team, her business partners and clients to drive consistent, recurring revenue for her company."

Notice this example's brevity. Keep in mind that personal branding statements should be brief and to the point. A paragraph (3-5 sentences) will often do the trick just fine.

You will notice that both of these examples are written in the third person (they) vs. the first person (I).

While it's okay to write a first person personal branding statement, third person remains the preferred point of view in the greater professional world. The good news is, it's very easy to craft a version of both first person and third person branding statements to have at the ready depending on the situation.

In short, a personal branding statement solidifies the essence of who you are and makes it clear to your target audience why they need you. It is the brief embodiment or essence of *you*: your passions, your dreams, your goals, your experiences and how all of them tied together can solve problems for others. It's what you leave behind in the minds and hearts of the people you touch long after you are no longer "in the room." It's both the tangible and the intangible of all that you are.

Chapter 2: Who Should Have a Personal Brand?

"All of us need to understand the importance of branding. We are CEOs of our own companies: Me, Inc. To be in business today, our most important job is to be the head marketer for the Brand Called You."
Tom Peters

In today's transparent business climate, everyone should have a personal brand. There really is no excuse for not investing some time into creating one for yourself. In fact, if you don't create your own personal brand, one will be created for you by default. I don't know about you, but I like to control what my brand is like.

Some examples of people who are creating personal brands include:

- Executive Business Leaders
- Sales Professionals
- Realtors
- Coaches
- Consultants
- Authors
- Teachers
- Managers
- Entrepreneurs
- CEOs

- Doctors
- Artists
- Journalists
- Students
- Athletes

And the list can go on from there.

Basically, any professional in the 21st century who wants more visibility and credibility for their business, organization, or message needs to develop a personal brand.

It truly is the calling card of the New Economy. It's not only what gets you noticed in the first place, but it also gets you remembered long after everyone else has moved on to the next thing.

In a world of 6-second Vine videos and people with the attention span of puppies in a dog park, getting noticed and then remembered is most of the battle right there.

Chapter 3: Why Do You Need a Personal Brand?

"Your brand is what people say about you when you're not in the room."
Jeff Bezos

Having a personal brand gives you power in a highly competitive marketplace. In today's robust business climate, and especially with the economy recovering from the shockwaves that hit in 2008, presenting yourself from a position of power and strength with a personal brand will only lead you to better opportunities for your career or business.

While it is never a guarantee that a personal brand will open every door for you, it is far better to have one than not to have one. People are attracted to people who know who they are and who present themselves with purpose and clarity. Employers, clients and business partners will find you far more appealing if you have a personal brand than if you don't.

Additionally, because the marketplace is so crowded and so competitive, setting yourself apart from the masses with a strategic personal brand will increase the chances that you will be remembered for the *right* reasons. Certainly, if you happen to be of the mind to be remembered for the wrong reasons, you can do that, too, and be just as effective.

A well-defined personal brand gives you an edge in positioning you and your offering – whether that is as an entrepreneur or an employee – over the folks who leave their personal branding up to the powers at be.

The key is to approach the process of creating your personal brand deliberately and purposefully. Own it no matter what, and the world will respond accordingly.

Chapter 4: How Do You Create a Personal Brand?

"Branding demands commitment; commitment to continual re-invention; striking chords with people to stir their emotions; and commitment to imagination. It is easy to be cynical about such things, much harder to be successful."
Sir Richard Branson

While there is no one step-by-step approach to creating a personal brand, there are some tried and true exercises that can lead you to identifying what specifically makes you unique. In Chapter 1, I shared a basic template for creating your personal branding statement. This chapter will get you thinking about some other questions that can lead you to solidifying that statement.

In order to succeed with this exercise, however, you need to forget about your job title or degree name for a moment and focus on one simple question:

What do you do that adds remarkable, measurable, distinguished, distinctive value to the audience you want to serve?

That's a deceptively simple question, one whose answer may not come to you immediately. Set aside a block of 15-30 minutes to write down as much as you can as you answer that question.

One way of approaching this exercise is with a Benjamin Franklin list.

On a piece of paper, create columns for each of the four words – remarkable, measurable, distinguished, and distinctive – and then list as many associations you can come up with for each word related to your experiences.

Furthermore, a personal branding statement often answers four key questions:

1. What makes you unique?
2. What distinguishes you from others?
3. Who is your target audience?
4. Why do you do what you do?

Resist using language that reflects climbing the corporate ladder or industry buzzwords that have no meaning outside a small circle of specialists. Really focus on the things that have made other people's lives better, small or big things, it really doesn't matter.

- Maybe you're the one who gets everyone laughing before a big meeting so they are more relaxed...
- Maybe you always close the deal, no matter what the challenges or obstacles...
- Maybe you always pack a healthy lunch for your kids to take to school...
- Maybe you're the person who always has something kind to say that makes people smile...

Another way of looking at this is with this question:

What have you accomplished that you can brag about?

Because the reality is, if you are going to be a brand, you have got to really focus on what you do that adds value, that you are proud of, and – arguably most importantly – that you can shamelessly take credit for.

This will not be easy as we are trained in this culture to be wary of bragging. But this is not a situation where your bragging will be obnoxious or offensive. It's all about driving down to the root of the **Brand Called You** so you can take those gold pieces you discover and begin designing your brand around them accordingly.

Chapter 5: How Do You Distinguish Your Brand from Everyone Else in Your Field?

"Your premium brand had better be delivering something special, or it's not going to get the business."
Warren Buffett

This is one of the most common questions about personal branding, and for good reason. Many people are in similar lines of work. For example, real estate agents, coaches, consultants, doctors, web designers, massage therapists, and marketers all operate within a competitive climate. With so many other people doing similar kinds of work or offering identical services, how do you set yourself apart from the rest?

One very effective way of distinguishing yourself from the rest of your field is to discover and then tell your signature story. A signature story is a story that you become known for and that you can use in many situations including job interviews, speaking engagements, and publicity events. What makes a story a far more compelling tool in your toolbox than other things comes down to something fundamental about all human beings: our brains are wired for stories and thus respond at a more visceral and lasting level.

Storytelling is the oldest form of communication and there is a reason it is a multi-billion dollar industry today. People – your prospects, your clients, your colleagues, your future boss – actually do want to know your story. Telling it immediately sets you apart from the pack because there is no one else in your profession with the same story, path, or background. There are several types or frameworks of signature stories to choose from.

What signature story you create will ultimately reflect your personality and the goals you have set for yourself. The best signature stories tend to be personal stories, ones that you lived. Stories based on your experiences allow you to recall details and share insights that will bring the story to life for your audience.

Two popular kinds of stories are 1. Vignettes and 2. Crucible stories.

A **vignette** is a short descriptive illustration, aka a mini story that is often crafted to illustrate a point. It often takes only a minute or two to tell, and isn't developed out with a lot of details. A vignette is the simplest and most common form of the business story. When crafted well, the vignette can pack a lot of punch.

A **crucible story** is one defined by great loss, suffering, or pain. It is often longer than a vignette, going into more detail so as to lead an audience along on the journey through the challenge you are recalling.

Cancer survivors, Olympic athletes, or anyone who has overcome nearly impossible odds tend to incorporate their signature crucible story into their personal brand, becoming known the world over for it.

Another popular framework for storytelling is based on Joseph Campbell's work with the Hero Myth. Each one of us is on our own heroic journey through life; the Hero Myth provides a fantastic template into which you can put elements of your personal journey.

I created a free training on how to use the Hero Myth as your secret weapon to generate a signature story that you can use in all sorts of situations including job interviews, speaking engagements, and networking events. Visit www.maryloukayser.com/vtsu to access this free training today.

At the end of the day, facts tell, stories sell. I know it's an old cliché, but there's a reason it's a cliché – it rings true.

And it works!

Chapter 6: How Much Does It Cost to Create a Personal Brand?

"Invest three percent of your income in yourself in order to guarantee your future."
Brian Tracy

The biggest investment you will make in creating your personal brand is your time. As I have pointed out several times already in this book, you will need to set aside some time to answer the questions in Chapter 4, and then brainstorm ideas based on the answers you come up with. You can do this work on your own, or you can hire a coach to help you go through the process. I have personally helped hundreds of people identify and refine their personal brands, and offer an exclusive discounted package for readers of this book.

Go to www.maryloukayser.com/pb to learn more.

The amount of money you choose to invest in developing and promoting your personal brand will be congruent with your goals. Some people start out with very little money, turning to close friends and associates to help them identify key elements of their brand. They then utilize the power of free Social Media sites like Facebook and Twitter to promote themselves and their personal brands to a larger audience.

Some people have the means to invest in hiring professional graphic designers and blog developers to help get their personal brands up and running quickly.

The beauty here is money and speed aren't necessarily prerequisites for success with personal branding. It is very possible to create a strong personal brand with next to no cash investment.

See Chapter 11 for some examples of people who have built remarkable personal brands through hard work, time, and perseverance that now pack significant social clout and punch.

Chapter 7: How Long Will It Take to Create Your Personal Brand?

"Patience, persistence and perspiration make an unbeatable combination for success."
Napoleon Hill

My research on this revealed the average turning point for recognizable personal brand creation seems to be about 6 months for most people who dedicate themselves consistently and deliberately to creating and promoting their personal brands.

What is meant by "recognizable" is when other people know your name and speak favorably of you and what you do for others. Some signs that you are gaining traction in this arena include:

- Your blog posts are getting comments on a more regular basis
- Your social media channels are growing with quality connections and increased engagement with your audience
- Your podcast is getting more downloads and reviews
- You are getting endorsements on LinkedIn and other spaces
- Your phone is ringing with referrals
- You are cashing more checks for your products or services

The Internet allows for this to happen much more quickly than at any other time in history. Despite the online world's accelerated pace, building a quality personal brand still takes time. Be patient as you work toward your goals of designing and delivering your personal brand.

It's easy to fall into what I call the "comparitis" trap when you see others out there who seem to have created their brand overnight and you're wondering why you can't seem to get any traction at all despite burning the candle at both ends.

Keep in mind that in almost every case with these success stories, many months and sometimes years are behind those successful personal brands you see blasted all over the web.

Stay focused, be patient, and keep the big picture in mind. Eventually, your personal brand will be one others who are just starting out will look to with amazement, awe, and respect.

Chapter 8: Is the Company You Work for Part of Your Personal Brand?

"You change the world by being yourself."
Yoko Ono

If you work for someone else, you are not your company, just as your company is not you. You may form an allegiance with that company while working for them, and that is certainly understandable.

But if you are an employee, one thing you must begin doing from this point forward is shifting your mindset from thinking like your company thinks to thinking like *you* think.

This is not to suggest that you cannot embrace the philosophies of your employer; many people do this and it's perfectly okay.

What I am saying is that from now, you must think of yourself as an independent person who is adding value to and solving problems for a company that resonates with *who you are and what you want to get done at this particular moment in time*. There is a big difference in these two ways of thinking.

And with the average person in America today having 14 different jobs BEFORE the age of 38, having your personal brand clear and well-defined is essential. The odds are greater than not that you will be moving around in your career – and taking your personal brand with you, NOT your previous company.

I like to use Phil Knight as an example here. Phil Knight is one of the original founders of Nike, and as such, is often equated with that company and all that it represents.

But Phil Knight is more than Nike, as he proves every day with his non-profit work into cancer research and other affiliations beyond the Nike campus.

If you are an entrepreneur, then the company you found will be a part of your personal brand, but the company itself will never be the Brand Called You. No matter what you do or where you go professionally, you will carry with you the essence of what makes you special and unique.

Those elements will always be more than one company could ever be.

Chapter 9: What's the First Thing You Should Do to Create Your Personal Brand?

"Create a website that expresses something about who you are that won't fit into the template available to you on a social networking site."
Jaron Lanier

Securing your personal piece of online real estate in the form of your name is arguably the first thing you should do when creating your personal brand.
The reason?

The world is moving online faster and faster with each passing day. Making sure you own your name on the Internet is critical. For less than $10 a year, you will know no one else can use your name for their gain. Note: If you have a name that is common, like "Mike Smith" or "Sue Davis" you can get creative with your name to set yourself apart from all the other Mike Smiths and Sue Davises out there. Consider the following examples:

> MeetMikeSmith.com
> Mike-Smith-Rocks.com
> WorkWithSueDavis.com

You can also see about buying a dot net version of your name if it's available.

The key is, **buy at least one piece of online real estate that is significant to your personal brand**. This domain will become the central hub of your problem-solving expertise, the place where you will send people and where people will find you.

While social media channels like Facebook, Twitter and LinkedIn are great places to set up for your personal brand, keep in mind that you don't own these spaces. Essentially, when you sign up for any social media account, you are signing a rental agreement with the owner of the respective platform. And while the most popular platforms are, for the most part, very generous to their renters, the only true piece of online real estate that you can own is a domain in your name or your business's name.

Be sure you are the owner of your personal brand's domain. If you invest in only one thing related to creating your personal brand, make sure it's this.

Chapter 10: What Are Some Examples of Regular People Who Have Successfully Created Their Personal Brands?

"Developing your personal brand is the same thing as living and breathing your resume every second that you're working."
Gary Vaynerchuk

There are an amazing number of everyday people who chose to follow their passion and make their lives better through building up their personal brands. Many of these people are entrepreneurs working on the Internet today who have organically built up powerful, celebrity-status personal brands through consistent efforts over time.

While the names I am about to list may not mean anything to you, they are good examples of ordinary folks who went after their dreams and in the process, created remarkable personal brands. I encourage you to Google their names and see what they are all about:

- Mari Smith
- James Wedmore
- John Lee Dumas
- Angelique Rewers
- Amy Porterfield
- Lori Morgan-Ferraro

- Sandy Krakowski
- Emma Tiebens
- Perry Marshall
- Darren Williger
- Kris Ruby
- Darren Hardy

Be sure to take a look at how each individual has branded him or herself online. Pay attention to their core message and how it is reflected in colors, images, website design, and the like.

For example, Mari Smith has done an excellent job of using the color turquoise to help define her personal brand. She is often photographed wearing turquoise clothes; her website has turquoise all over it, as do her books and videos.

Also look at their social profiles to get a sense of how they carry their personal brand from one place to the next. Many of these people are leveraging the power of technology through blogs, videos, podcasts, speaking engagements, and social media to broadcast their brand with lightning speed. Consistency is key with personal branding, and the people on this list have figured that out.

Chapter 11: What Benefits Will Having a Personal Brand Give You?

"Follow your bliss and the Universe will open doors where there were only walls."
Joseph Campbell

Having a personal brand will benefit you in numerous ways. Some of the more common benefits you can expect from developing your personal brand include:

- Opening doors to new opportunities and alliances in your area of expertise
- Moving your company forward
- Reducing the amount of time in a sales cycle (i.e. faster profits!)
- Increasing the "Q" factor of your life exponentially – adding more *quality* to everything you do

As you build your career and your business, you want people to remember you for the value you add to their lives. With each step along the way, you are adding pieces to the overall personal branding puzzle called you. Remember, it won't come overnight. Personal branding is a **process**, one that requires strategic planning and consistency.

The more you become visible, and the more you become known for the value you give to the world, the more you will receive back from the people you most want to serve.

It is such an amazing experience to meet new people who already feel like they know your best self because of the personal branding work you have done.

In fact, I can't think of a greater feeling than the one that comes when you receive a phone call or email from someone you don't know who has learned about you through a friend or colleague and wants you to help them solve their problem.

Chapter 12: Do You Need to Have Professional Photos Taken of Yourself?

"Photography deals exquisitely with appearances, but nothing is what it appears to be."
Duane Michals

Do you need to have professional photos taken of yourself?

Not necessarily, but...

I recommend doing it. Having at least one high quality head shot is something professionals in many areas have been doing for years. Actors and models are just one of many examples. In this era of personal branding, everyone needs to have a decent photo to use in marketing and promotional materials, both online and offline.

Of all the online sites you might use for your personal brand, LinkedIn is the one that practically demands you have a quality photo of yourself. With an average annual income of $108,000, LinkedIn users aren't going to be as receptive to a cropped shot of you on the beach holding an umbrella drink or perhaps even worse – no photo at all. I make it a personal rule not to accept any LinkedIn connection requests from people who either have no photo or a photo of poor quality or poor judgment. Both of these situations tell me more than any words ever could.

The good news is, these days many people own super slick high resolution digital SLR cameras (like the Nikon D40 or the Canon EOS). And mobile devices like iPhones and Samsungs take remarkable pictures. If you have a friend or relative who owns one of these devices and has an eye for lighting and setting, I'd be willing to bet you can trade a home cooked meal (or some other good or service) for an hour or two photo shoot session.

Many of the photos I use currently are ones from photo sessions I've done with family members and friends who have professional-level photography skills. One benefit of having a friend take your pictures for you rather than paying for a studio session is you can get a LOT more photos – usually for free, or some kind of trade or barter.

A delicious meal can also go a long way. If you are just starting out, don't be afraid to explain your situation and find out if they are open to alternative forms of payment. You'd be surprised at how many people are happy to help for a homemade cake.

In one particular photo shoot, my friend Lesley shot more than 100 pictures of me, and I have every one stored on both a disc and my hard drive. I love having a variety of options to choose from. Plus I don't have to worry about violating copyright laws, although most professional studios these days offer in their packages an Internet option where you have the rights to upload their photo of you to any site online.

Just be sure you aren't plastering "selfies" all over the place. The shots many people enjoy taking of themselves using their Smartphones are a lot of fun – especially when you can get one with someone famous.

But unless your personal brand is somehow tied to the "selfie" culture, steer away from using one for your professional marketing collateral. Keep those fun shots of you hanging out on the beach in Cabo with JayZ or the ball park with Peyton Manning on your private profile pages where friends and family can comment and enjoy.

Chapter 13: How Will Blogging Help Your Personal Brand?

"My site has the whole thing - blogs, information, video interviews."
William Shatner

Blogging continues to be a solid method of building a personal brand, so if you do not yet have a personal blog, I encourage you to get one. Like, right now.

And you don't have to like writing to have a successful blog or website, either. There are tons of people who choose to create short videos and upload them to their blog instead of writing posts. The point is to consistently add content that enhances and solidifies your personal brand.

In his best-selling book *Linchpin*, Seth Godin predicts that the traditional resume will soon be extinct, replaced instead with personal blogs and other pieces of important online real estate individuals create. These will become the sources of information for potential employers and/or business partners to learn more about you and what you can do to solve their problems.

Having a personal blog gives you credibility, as well as a place to interact with others. It is a terrific portal through which key relationships with like-minded individuals can begin and develop.

It is a place where you can post your thoughts and insights about subjects related directly to your business, and by default, add more credibility to your emerging personal brand.

Over time, your blog will become your calling card for anyone wanting to know more about you and what you value. It will be the central hub of the Brand Called You.

These days, getting a blog or website up and running takes hours, not weeks. As with any other business decision, take the time to identify what you want your blog or website to look like so it is aligned from the start with your personal brand. I recommend looking at the blogs or websites of people in your industry to get a sense of design and presentation.

Then, either get a referral for a web designer from someone you trust or invest the time to learn how to set up a site yourself. Most people find they would rather invest some money to have their blog built right from the start than go through the steep learning curve involved with building a decent site.

One word of caution: beware one-size-fits-all shops that advertise on TV with big promises about getting a website up and running. There are a lot of factors to consider when building your online real estate.

Consult with experts and get several perspectives before racing out of the starting gate. Take it from someone who's been there – the extra time you take before getting a site up and running is well worth it in the long run.

Should you have any questions about getting your blog or website up and running, I invite you to connect with me on my social media sites. You can find addresses to where I hang out online at the end of this book.

I am happy to answer your questions and offer a free initial 15-minute consultation with new people who are truly invested in moving their personal branding efforts forward.

Chapter 14: What Matters More in Personal Branding: What You Look Like or What You Can Do?

"Real generosity toward the future lies in giving all to the present."
Albert Camus

There is no denying that we live in a culture where looks do matter. And while America tends to be more youth-obsessed than other countries, there is always room in the marketplace for people of all ages with value to share.

With the explosion of YouTube and other video hosting platforms in recent years, a lot of business today is relying on online video to broadcast messages, promotions, and educational material for their target audience. Given the rise of video in the marketplace, how you present yourself to the world visually is important. But as a professional, you always want to put your best self forward regardless of the delivery system.

That said, you do not have to be a movie star with perfect hair and lips and twelve pack abs! Nor do you have to be twenty years old or a size 0 or look like you spend every second of your life in the weight room.

When you present yourself publicly, you want to be the best *you* possible. On the day you have your photos taken or record your videos, be sure you are groomed nicely.

Beyond that, ultimately what matters most in creating a powerful personal brand is what you do for others. Delivering on your promises. Following through. Keeping appointments. Demonstrating a passion for your business, as well as for the audience you or your business serves. Helping others get results.

The success of your personal brand will boil down to how much people feel you care about them and what they want to get done. All the pretty pictures and videos and whistles and bells can never replace good old-fashioned caring – that comes from the heart, that is genuine.

Some of the most successful people in the world are not movie star gorgeous – and some of the most physically attractive people are terribly selfish and care only about what's in it for them at that moment. Be polished. Be professional. But most importantly, be generous. More than anything else, generosity will increase your personal brand quotient exponentially. And getting a reputation as someone who gives more than they take will have people talking about you for all the right reasons, which is exactly what you want!

Chapter 15: How Do You Get Other People to Talk about You and Endorse Your Personal Brand?

"Social media is called social media for a reason. It lends itself to sharing rather than horn-tooting."
Margaret Atwood

Once people you do not know are talking about you – once that "buzz" is humming across the social media sites about you and what you do – you will know you have successfully secured the Brand Called You.

Athletes and celebrities are paid enormous amounts of money by companies looking to increase the buzz about their products and add credibility to their goods and services. Think of Michael Jordan and Hanes tee shirts... Derek Jeter and Gillette razors... Bono and the non-profit organization ONE... Jennifer Hudson and Weight Watchers.

Some experts are suggesting that we are entering an era of everyday endorsements, where regular folks act as affiliates for a host of goods and services, reaping rewards from affiliate sales and the likes, just as celebrities have been enjoying for years.

Just as a car company seeks out a high profile person to use in television commercials, so should you find people who are willing to give you two thumbs up for what you do.

Testimonies can come in a variety of forms, from written comments on a blog to a video post by a client who raves about your work. Endorsements do several important things for your personal brand, including adding social proof to who you are. Because of this, you want to choose the best ones wisely.

I will never forget the day when one of my own online heroes – John Lee Dumas, host of the Entrepreneur on Fire Podcast – not only retweeted some of my posts, but started following me on Twitter.

John is well-respected in the online entrepreneurial space, as well as a major podcaster, so to have him notice my activity and be a part of my social media network was very exciting. That's when I knew I was getting somewhere with my tweeting efforts and the buzz was beginning to really hum.

Chapter 16: What Social Media Sites Should You Use for Your Personal Brand?

*"Companies can't beat real people on social media.
They have to join them."*
Jay Baer

Of course, you will want to set up accounts with all the biggies:

- Facebook (both personal and professional pages)
- Twitter
- LinkeIn
- YouTube
- Google +
- Pinterest
- Instagram

You will also want to consider using these lesser-known but emerging social media sites:

- Skype
- Wikipedia

And you also will want to create a Gravatar that will appear next to any comments you write on other people's sites (which you will be doing as part of building up your personal brand). If possible, use the same photograph you're using for all your other sites so that you begin to create a consistent "image trail" around the Internet.

To learn more about how to create a Gravatar, visit http://en.gravatar.com/site/signup and follow the instructions.

Don't let that list of social media sites paralyze you. There is no law that says every personal brand has to be on every big social media site. I list the biggies here because it wouldn't be fair to leave some names out based on my personal biases.

I will confess that I do not actively post to every social media channel on that list, but instead have selected the ones that give me the greatest return on my time investment (ROTI).

It took me awhile to learn through experiment with the different channels which ones were going to suit my needs best. After several tests, I discovered I was getting the most engagement from Twitter, Facebook, and LinkedIn. Like anything else in life, you get out of social media what you put in.

I recommend you do the same. If you aren't sure where to start, check out what 3-5 of the folks you most admire in your area of expertise are doing. That may provide some fast insights for you and save you some time in the long run.

The bottom line with the Internet and Social Media is this. For now, at least, you are what Google says you are, so you might as well control that information as best you can and put your best foot forward always, no matter which channel(s) turn out to make the most sense for you and your goals.

Chapter 17: What Are the ~~3~~ 4 Best Ways to Increase Visibility of Your Personal Brand Online?

"If you don't get noticed, you don't have anything. You just have to be noticed, but the art is in getting noticed naturally, without screaming or without tricks."

Leo Burnett

This list is based on my personal experience, and should be taken as such. It is by no means THE definitive list, but rather one that has worked exceptionally well for me and people I know:

- Create a blog or website in your name
- Use video whenever possible
- Be an active member on the big social media sites (see previous chapter)
- Start a podcast

I want to take a minute and briefly talk about the fourth and most recently added item on this list: podcasting. Arguably, how you present yourself visually to your audience is an enormous part of the personal branding equation. Most people will say they learn best when they can see something. This is one of the reasons why video is so popular online.

But what you *sound* like can have a big impact on growing your personal brand as well, so it's something you may want to consider adding to your personal branding strategy at some point.

The master of teaching podcasting strategies is John Lee Dumas. You can learn more about John on his website at www.entrepreneuronfire.com . Of anyone building a personal brand through the podcasting medium, John is it.

In the grand scheme of things, any activity you do online is recorded, so the sooner you get going with your online branding efforts, the better off you will be on building awareness about you. It's a lot like a savings account or an exercise program: A little bit each day or week adds up fast. Don't wait until conditions are "perfect." Make a list of all you need to do and give yourself some time to work through that list until everything is checked off and your branding portals are ready to go.

Also, you don't have to master or dominate every social media channel to build your personal brand. Many very successful people who have created exceptional personal brands focus their attention on one or two channels. The key is they post often and on purpose, and what they post invites engagement from the people who choose to follow them.

Create and share high quality content with great value to your target audience and your personal brand will become a fixture in their minds in relatively no time.

Chapter 18: What Are Some Ways You Can Promote Your Personal Brand Offline?

"Without promotion, something terrible happens... nothing!"

P. T. Barnum

With all the buzz these days surrounding the Internet and Social Media, traditional offline activities where people gather live and in person like Chamber of Commerce meetings and Rotary Club presentations have been overshadowed.

The truth is, at some point you will have to take your personal brand offline and meet people face to face. After all, people do business with people, not things! Live events are still by far one of the best ways to promote yourself and expose people to your personal brand. Here is a list of suggestions for getting yourself "out there," belly-to-belly:

- Local Workshops
- Conferences
- After-Hours Networking Events
- Chamber of Commerce Meetings
- Author Book Tours
- Live Lectures
- Local Meet Ups
- Alumni Chapter Events
- Leads Groups

- Community Service Opportunities

Local papers and online sites like Eventbrite.com, Meetup.com and Craigslist Local Events can provide an ongoing list of live events going on in an area each week. Facebook and Twitter are also great resources for finding live events that could be worth your time to attend.

Always carry with you something you can give away that is branded for you. Business cards are still the most popular item, but you can think beyond the card here if you want to set yourself apart. One gesture that will make you stand out from the pack is offering people access codes for a free download of an eBook you've written or a promotional post card for a discounted or free offer on products or services you have.

I have even known people to give away copies of their books with their business card glued in the front of the book!

You are limited only by your imagination at live events, just as you are online. The bottom line is to come from a place of service and generosity, not pitching or spamming. Connect with folks from the heart. Prove you have something of value to offer and then find ways of sharing it.

Finally, connect with people you meet at these events after the event is over. Within an hour of getting home after being at something live, I pull out the stack of business cards I collected and send a quick, personal note to each person on LinkedIn, with a request to add them to my professional network. This activity alone has allowed me to build connections with a lot of powerful people.

9 times out of 10, after returning from a live event, most people simply take all the cards, brochures and flyers they collected and dump them on their desk, never to be looked at again. This, to me, is a tremendous waste, not to mention a lost opportunity.

I know of one woman who makes a point of either writing a personal thank you note and sending it in the mail or calling and leaving a voice mail to every single person she gets a business card from at a live event. And you know what? She has built a powerful personal brand because of this. People remember her because she cared enough to connect beyond the initial meeting.

Remember, people don't care how much you know until they know how much you care about them and their problems. At the end of the day, each of us is looking for genuine connections. Make a point of being one of the few who actually is sincere about the new relationships you build with others.

Chapter 19: How Do You Manage Everything Related to Creating Your Personal Brand?

"I always tell my kids if you lay down, people will step over you. But if you keep scrambling, if you keep going, someone will always, always give you a hand. Always. But you gotta keep dancing, you gotta keep your feet moving."
Morgan Freeman

Everyone who is new to creating a personal brand gets overwhelmed at some point during the process. There just seems to be too many things to manage all at once.

In one of the funniest movies I have ever seen called "What about Bob?" Bill Murray's character "Bob" struggles with moving forward in his life. The psychiatrist he is referred to (after getting "fired" from another psychiatrist) has written and is promoting a book called "Baby Steps," which he immediately recommends Bob reads. Bob takes Dr. Marvin's advice to heart, following the recommendations in the book to the letter.

While what happens next is the stuff of fantastic comedy, the lesson is clear: small steps taken every day over time often yield big results. Just like in this movie, baby steps are your friend when it comes to personal branding.

Nike wasn't built in a day. Neither was Celine Dion or Oprah or Ellen DeGeneres.

Be patient with yourself as you navigate through each stage of personal branding development. If you are consistently doing things that add value to who you are and to others, you will create a rock solid, definitive personal brand.

The best advice I can offer at this point is to not try to do everything related to building your personal brand all by yourself. Seek help. Getting help will make the process less stressful for you, and besides -- it's also a lot more fun when you are on the journey with others.

Your personal brand will eventually all come together (remember that 6 month tipping point!) and you will wake up one day and realize your personal brand is not only making waves, but making a difference in other's lives, too in ways you never imagined. Be open to the process, and it will reward you.

Chapter 20: What Are Some Other Resources on Personal Branding?

As the economy continues to shift and expand, especially into the mobile market, personal branding will become more commonplace. Just Google the phrase "personal branding" and you get back more than 1 million *exact* results!

The following is a list of some credible sources of information about personal branding that I have used. Because this topic is just gaining momentum, there aren't many sources I would consider reputable...yet. This list represents resources I can recommend with 100% confidence.

Online Resources

Natasha Hazlett = www.natashahazlett.com
Dan Schwabel = www.danschwabel.com
William Arruda = www.reachpersonalbranding.com
Kris Ruby = www.rubymediagroup.com

Recommended Books

Branding for Dummies by Barbara Findley Schenck
Purple Cow by Seth Godin
Linchpin by Seth Godin
Good to Great by Jim Collins (pay close attention to what he calls "The Hedgehog Concept")
The Compound Effect by Darren Hardy

The People Code: It's All About Your Innate Motive by Taylor Hartman
How the World Sees You: Discover Your Highest Value through the Science of Fascination by Sally Hogshead
Now Go Discover Your Strengths by Marcus Buckingham

Recommended Podcasts

John Lee Dumas = www.entrepreneuronfire.com
John Cote = www.healthcareelsewhere.com
Kim Doyal = www.thewpchick.com/podcast/
Amy Porterfield = www.amyporterfield.com/category/podcast/
Michael Stelzner = www.socialmediaexaminer.com/category/podcast-episodes/
Mary Lou Kayser = www.pyppodcast.com

Final Thoughts

If you found this book at all valuable, please share it with someone you know who could benefit from this information. Tweet about it, share it on Facebook, send someone on your email list a link to it, lend it to another reader. They will be so glad you thought of them!

We live in an age where transparency and authenticity are driving forces behind all successful people. Doing what it takes to identify and build your personal branding foundation will do wonders for your profession and your business.

The online world and the offline world are becoming more blurred each day, which is why it is so important to design your personal brand strategically.

As a special bonus for readers of this book, **I am offering an exclusive discount on my personal branding coaching packages for anyone who wants additional help with putting together your personal brand.**

Believe me – I know how overwhelming this process can be. I was grateful for the professional help I got when putting together my own personal brand in those early days of building my business.

Simply visit www.maryloukayser.com/pb to take advantage of this special no-risk offer today!

Now is YOUR time to step up and step out into your amazing, remarkable self!

I look forward to sharing the journey with you.

To your highest and best,

Mary Lou Kayser, May 2014
Portland, Oregon

Let's Connect!

Are we connected yet online?

Find me on social media:

https://twitter.com/MaryLouKayser
https://www.facebook.com/ForwardMotion
https://www.linkedin.com/in/mlkayser

Visit my websites:

www.maryloukayser.com
www.pyppodcast.com

Email me:

mlk@maryloukayser.com

Gratitude

Just as a quarterback can't win a championship game alone, nor can an author write a book by herself. I feel very fortunate to have an incredible circle of close friends and family who not only support my writing efforts, but offer me candid feedback on my manuscripts.

To Mom and Dad, who have been my biggest cheerleaders from the start. Your ongoing love and support have allowed me to pursue my dreams and be fully who I am.

To Susie Kanewske, for listening to my ideas and encouraging me to keep going no matter what. And for making sure I always look my best while crafting my next manifesto.

To the folks at Createspace and Kindle who allow authors like me to make our publishing dreams come true.

And to my Pilot, for not only catching those last-minute typos and missed words at the 11th hour, but for believing in me no matter what. I appreciate your steadfast love and support in more ways than words can express.

About the Author

Mary Lou Kayser, M.A.T. is a well-respected business strategist, coach, author, trainer, and speaker dedicated to helping leaders make forward progress in today's accelerated marketplace with agility, innovation, and speed. She is the Founder & CEO of The Kingfisher Group and host of the Play Your Position Podcast, a show that celebrates leadership, achievement, and mastery. Mary Lou earned a Masters Degree from Lewis and Clark College and a B.A. from the University of Puget Sound. She lives in Beaverton, Oregon with her family including her two children and two cats. Meet Mary Lou and learn how she can help you and your team at www.maryloukayser.com

Personal Branding Secrets for Beginners

Made in the USA
Charleston, SC
12 May 2016